MY NATURE CRAFT BOOK

MY NATURE CRAFT BOOK

Cheryl Owen

LITTLE, BROWN AND COMPANY
BOSTON   TORONTO   LONDON

First Edition

Library of Congress Cataloging-in-Publication Data

Owen, Cheryl.
    My naturecrafts book/Cheryl Owen. — 1st ed.
        p. cm.
    Summary: Provides instructions for over thirty-five craft projects
using a selection of natural materials.
    ISBN–0–316–67715–9
    1. Nature craft—Juvenile literature. [1. Nature craft.
2. Handicraft.] I. Title.
TT160.084 1993
745.5—dc20   92-10187

10 9 8 7 6 5 4 3 2 1

Produced by Salamander Books Limited,
129-137 York Way, London N7 9LG, England.

CREDITS

Managing editor: Veronica Ross
Art director: Rachael Stone
Photographer: Jonathan Pollock
Assistant photographer: Peter Cassidy
Additional designs by: Alan Dart and Caroline Green
Editor: Coral Walker
Designer: Anita Ruddell
Illustrator: Stan North
Character illustrator: Jo Gapper
Diagram artist: Malcolm Porter
Typeset by: Ian Palmer
Color separation by: P & W Graphics, Pte., Singapore

Special thanks to Judy Taylor for her
contributions to this book.

Published simultaneously in Canada
by Little, Brown & Company (Canada) Limited

Printed in Italy

CONTENTS

INTRODUCTION

Today people everywhere are becoming more interested in their natural surroundings. *My Nature Craft Book* will show you how to create a wide selection of pretty and practical objects from things you can find in the country or on the beach, even in your own backyard or local park. Each project is fun to make, and the clearly illustrated, step-by-step instructions are easy to follow. The end results are so attractive that no one will believe your craft is homemade!

MATERIALS AND EQUIPMENT

When out on walks or on the beach, look for things you can collect and use later: shells, stones, old driftwood, or fallen tree bark and pine cones. Do not pick wild flowers without first asking an adult. Although some flowers are plentiful, many types are now threatened with extinction. You can also ask your parents or a friend if there any plants in the garden that you could pick to press or dry.

Also look around your home for things to recycle: string, old boxes, or scraps of leftover fabric. Remember to save cereal boxes, as they are a great source of cardboard. Tubes from paper towel or toilet paper rolls make great napkin rings. And dried herbs past their prime are perfect for bath sachets.

BEFORE YOU BEGIN

- Check with an adult before starting any project; you might need some help.
- Read through the instructions before you begin.
- Gather together everything you need first.
- Cover the work surface with an old sheet or newspaper.
- Protect your clothes with an apron or wear old clothes.

WHEN YOU HAVE FINISHED

- Replace the tops on glue and pens, wash paintbrushes and your hands.
- Put everything away. Store pens, paints, glue, etc. in old ice cream tubs, coffee cans, or cookie tins.

SAFETY FIRST!

You will be able to make most of the projects in this book yourself. However, some of the designs involve sharp scissors or an oven, and these projects have been marked with a SAFETY TIP. Do use common sense when using anything sharp or hot and ask an adult for help.

Read the instructions thoroughly before you begin.

USING PATTERNS

At the back of the book you will find the patterns you will need for some of the projects. Using a pencil, trace the pattern you need onto tracing paper. If you are making a project with fabric, cut the pattern out and pin it to the fabric. Cut out the shape. If you want to cut the pattern out of poster board, turn your tracing over and rub firmly over the pattern outline with a pencil. The pattern will transfer on to the poster board. Cut out this shape.

Once you have gained confidence making some of the projects, go on to adapt the ideas to create your own designs. If you enjoy drawing, try making up your own patterns freehand.

GROWNUPS TAKE NOTE

Every project in *My Nature Craft Book* has been designed with simplicity, yet effectiveness, in mind. However, occasionally sharp scissors or an oven will be needed. Your involvement will depend on the age and ability of the child, but we do recommend that you read through each project before it is undertaken.

And please remember these basic rules of safety:

- Never leave scissors open or lying around where smaller children can reach them.

- Always stick needles and pins into a pin cushion or a scrap of cloth when you are not using them.

- Never use an oven or a sharp knife without the help or supervision of an adult.

Never use an oven or a sharp knife without the help of an adult.

Some wild flowers are scarce. Check with an adult before you pick any.

LEAF PRINT PAPER

YOU WILL NEED
Old newspaper
Leaves
Poster paints
Paintbrush
Paper
Wax crayons
Scissors
Narrow ribbon
All-purpose glue
Scotch tape

Next time you are out on a walk, collect lots of different-shaped leaves. With them you can practice making your own leaf print wrapping paper. Use the paper and the matching tags to make very original-looking gifts.

1 Cover your work surface with old newspaper. To make a print, carefully paint one side of a leaf with poster paint.

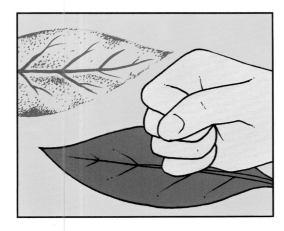

2 Lay the leaf face down on a sheet of paper. Press the leaf down firmly with your fist. Remove the leaf and repeat to make another print. Once the paint on the paper is dry, you can wrap your present.

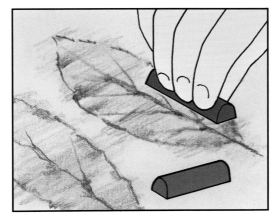

3 To make a gift tag, place a leaf under a sheet of paper. Rub a wax crayon over the paper until you see the leaf image appear. Cut out the leaf shape.

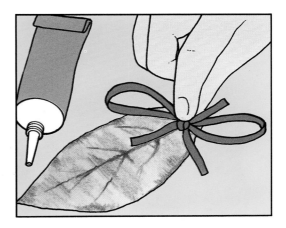

4 To finish, tie a ribbon bow and glue it to the tag. Write your message on the back of the tag and tape it onto the wrapped present.

SUMMER HATS

Miniature straw hats look stunning
when they are decorated with tiny
bunches of dried flowers and ribbons.
Try decorating a whole range of
different-sized hats and hang them
on your bedroom wall.

YOU WILL NEED
Miniature straw hats
(from craft store)
All-purpose glue
Lace edging
Dried flowers
Thread
Narrow ribbon

1 Carefully glue a length of lace under the brim of a straw hat. Make sure that the decorative edge faces outward.

2 Tie tiny bunches of dried flowers together with cotton thread. Arrange them around the crown of the hat.

3 Glue the flowers in place. You can glue on a single bunch, or cover the whole brim of the hat with flowers.

4 To finish, tie narrow ribbon into a bow and glue it to the hat. Trim the ends of the ribbon.

PRESSED FLOWER CARDS

Pick flowers and leaves during the summer and press them to use as decorations for cards, gift tags, and pictures. Flat daisy shapes press well, as do grasses, leaves, and ferns.

1 Place the flowers and leaves on blotter paper. Fold the paper over to cover them and press the flowers between the pages of a heavy book.

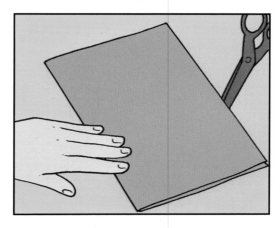

2 After a few weeks, carefully remove the flowers and leaves. Cut a rectangle of colored poster board and fold it in half to make a greeting card.

3 Arrange the flowers and leaves in a pretty design on the front of the card.

YOU WILL NEED

Assorted flowers and leaves
Blotter paper
Heavy book
Scissors
Poster board
All-purpose glue
Clear sticky-backed
  plastic (from art
  or craft store)

4 Carefully glue all the pieces to the card. You can cover the cards with clear sticky-backed plastic to protect the flowers from being damaged.

COCKATIEL COLLAGE

Pressed flowers and silvery honesty seed heads work well together to make colorful collages. Follow the instructions here to make this exotic cockatiel, or try drawing your own designs.

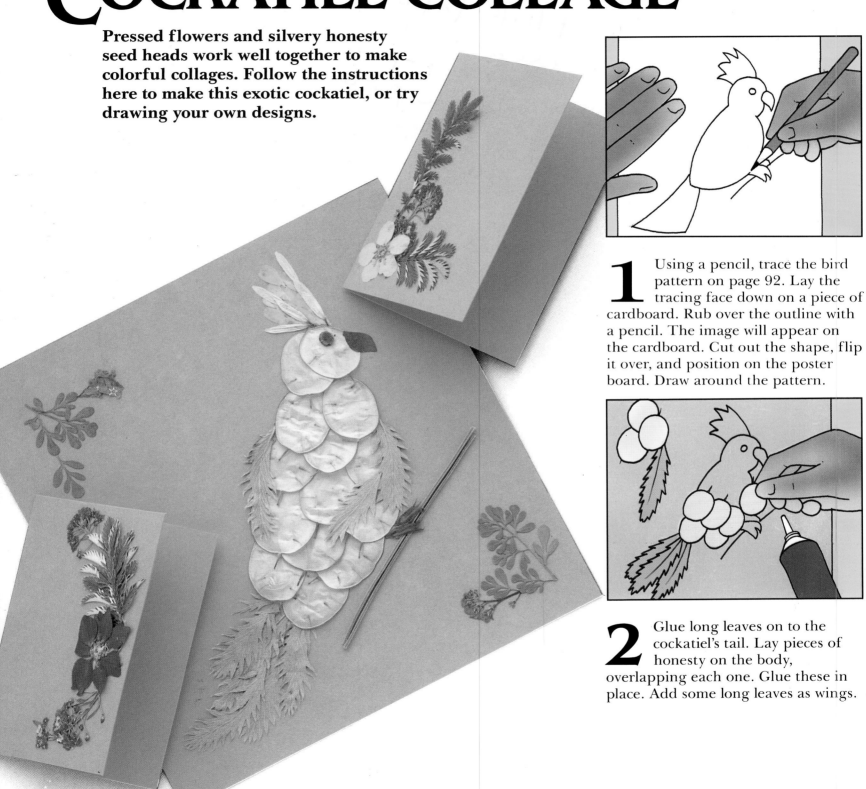

1 Using a pencil, trace the bird pattern on page 92. Lay the tracing face down on a piece of cardboard. Rub over the outline with a pencil. The image will appear on the cardboard. Cut out the shape, flip it over, and position on the poster board. Draw around the pattern.

2 Glue long leaves on to the cockatiel's tail. Lay pieces of honesty on the body, overlapping each one. Glue these in place. Add some long leaves as wings.

3 For the beak, glue on a small leaf and for the eye use the center of a small flower. Glue on the stick to look like a perch and then glue on two little leaves as feet.

4 Make the crest on the cockatiel's head from yellow and white petals. Complete the picture by glueing small groups of leaves in two corners of the poster board.

YOU WILL NEED
Tracing paper
   and pencil
Cardboard
Colored poster board
Pressed flowers and leaves
Honesty (money plant)
   seed heads
All-purpose glue
Small stick

ANIMAL SEED PICTURES

These animal collages are made from seeds and grasses. These instructions explain how to make the squirrel, but the badger is made in the same way. You can also try drawing your own animal shapes to make a set of woodland collages.

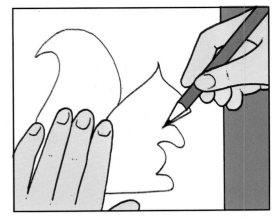

1 Using a pencil, trace the animal patterns on page 93. Lay the tracings face down on a piece of cardboard. Rub firmly over the outlines with a pencil. The patterns will appear on the cardboard. Cut out the shapes, flip them over, and position on the green poster board. Draw around the animal patterns.

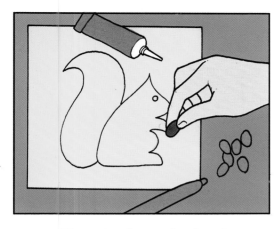

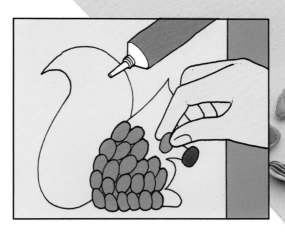

2 To make the squirrel, color pumpkin seeds bright orange using a felt-tip pen. Break a hazelnut in half and glue it to the squirrel's paw.

3 Overlap the seeds within the body shape and glue them in place. Stick a split pea on the face as an eye.

4 Glue red-colored grasses to the squirrel's tail and other colored grasses along the edges of the poster board.

YOU WILL NEED
Tracing paper and pencil
Green poster board
Thin cardboard
Sunflower and
   pumpkin seeds
Orange felt-tip pen
Hazelnut or acorn
All-purpose glue
A few split peas
Colored grasses

LEAF LADY

Gather some autumn leaves and grasses from your yard or local park and make this pretty collage. The leaf lady would make a perfect gift for a friend with an autumn birthday.

1 Using a pencil, trace the pattern on page 94. Turn the tracing over and lay it on a sheet of firm paper. Rub firmly over the outline with a pencil. The leaf lady pattern will appear on the paper. Use colored pencils to add the face details.

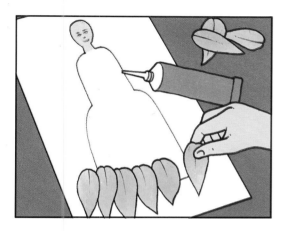

3 Use smaller, different colored leaves for the bodice, and long thin leaves for the arms. Glue these in place carefully.

2 Use the largest leaves to make the leaf lady's skirt. Start at the hem and work up. Glue the tips of the leaves in place.

4 Finally, glue on some rat's tail statice for hair and put some leaves or ears of wheat in the leaf lady's arms.

YOU WILL NEED
Tracing paper and pencil
Firm paper
Colored pencils
Leaves and grasses
Rat's tail statice
All-purpose glue

STRING PRINTS

Use rope, string, or natural materials, such as bark, to make all sorts of interesting patterns with block prints. We have used string blocks to decorate table mats, a scarf, and some notepaper, but you can print almost anything.

1 To make a block, carefully cut a piece of thick cardboard about 1½ inch x 3 inch.

2 Take a short length of string and coil it into an interesting shape, glueing it to the block as you work. Allow it to dry.

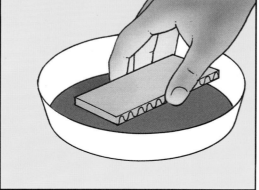

3 Dilute the paint with a little water and pour it into a shallow dish. Dip the string block into the paint.

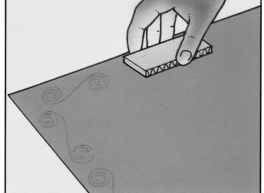

4 Shake off any excess paint and press the string block firmly on to the fabric or paper to make a print. Do not use too much paint or the pattern and texture of the string will be lost.

LAVENDER BAGS

Make these delightful scented bags from scraps of pink, blue, or lavender-colored fabric filled with sweet-smelling lavender. Store the bags among your clothes to keep them smelling fresh.

1 Using pinking shears, cut out a rectangle of fabric roughly 7 x 5½ inches.

YOU WILL NEED
Pinking shears
Scraps of fabric
Needle and thread
Dried lavender
(from drug store or
beauty shop)
Ribbon

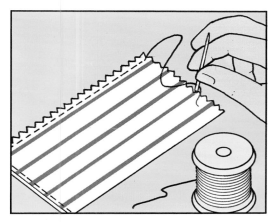

2 Fold the rectangle in half widthwise so that the right side of the fabric is facing in. Sew along the bottom edge and the side edge, as shown.

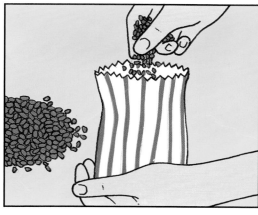

3 Turn the bag the right way out and fill it with a few handfuls of dried lavender.

4 To finish, tie a length of ribbon in a tight bow around the neck of the bag.

FRUIT POMANDERS

Smelling lightly of citrus and cloves, these fruit pomanders look especially pretty in the kitchen or bedroom, hanging from bright, cheerful ribbons.

YOU WILL NEED
Oranges and lemons
1-inch wide ribbon
Cloves

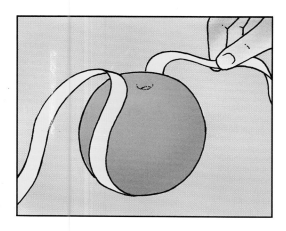

1 Fold a length of ribbon in half lengthwise. Place the fruit on the ribbon and bring the two ends of the ribbon up around the fruit.

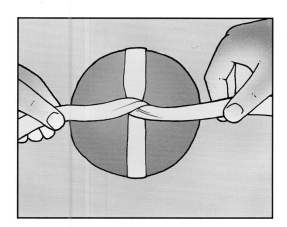

2 Where the ribbon meets at the top of the fruit, twist the two lengths of ribbon together, as shown. Take the ribbon back around the fruit and tie in a bow.

3 If you prefer, wrap the ribbon around the fruit just once. Tie a bow on top and trim the ends of the ribbon neatly.

4 Now decorate the fruit with cloves. Push them into the skin of the fruit, either in a pattern, or covering the surface completely.

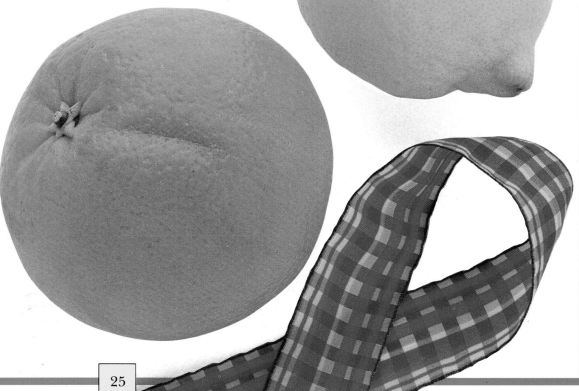

PAINTED STONES

Painted stones make pretty decorations
and great vacation souvenirs. Next time
you are at the beach collect some smooth
stones to decorate when you get home.

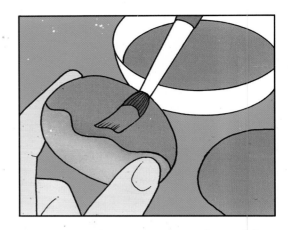

1 Cover your work surface with old newspaper. Wash the stones and allow them to dry overnight. Paint on the blue background color.

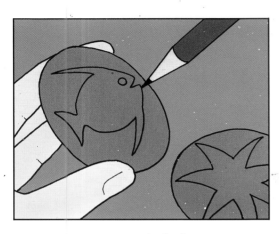

2 Draw a rough design on a piece of scrap paper. When you are happy with your picture, draw the outline on the stone.

3 Following the outline of your design, carefully fill in the details with paint. Allow the stones to dry in a safe place.

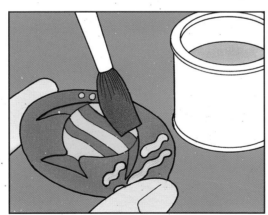

4 To keep your painted stones looking fresh and bright, coat your design with craft varnish, using a paintbrush.

YOU WILL NEED
Old newspaper
Smooth stones
Poster paints
Paintbrush
Pencil
Scrap paper
Craft varnish
    (from craft or
        hardware store)

FANTASY TREES

These weird and wonderful trees "grow" from poster paints. The natural-looking designs can make very unusual cards, pictures, and gift tags. Follow the instructions here, or try creating your own original designs.

1 Using the natural sponge, dampen both sides of the watercolor paper with water. Stick the paper on to a flat surface with gummed paper tape. This stops the paper from curling when wet. Smooth out any creases with the sponge.

2 When the paper is dry, dampen a small natural sponge and dip it into a small dish of watery blue-green paint. Dab the sponge over the paper to create the background.

YOU WILL NEED
Old newspaper
Watercolor paper
Gummed paper tape
Small natural sponge
Poster paints
   diluted with water
Small dish
Eye-dropper
Drinking straw

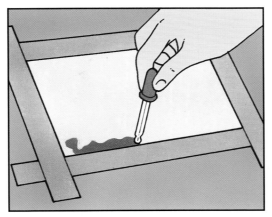

3 Using an eye-dropper, carefully drop runny black or brown paint along the bottom of the paper.

4 Blow hard through a drinking straw while the paint is still wet to make the trees grow.

TEDDY BEAR CANDLE HOLDERS

These cute teddy bear candle holders are perfect for any birthday party. They are made from salt-dough, which can be made from basic ingredients in the kitchen cupboard. The ingredients here make one bear.

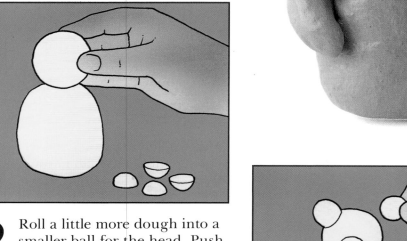

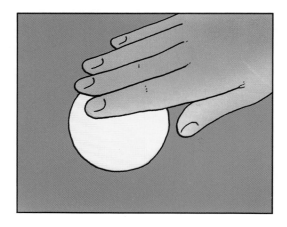

1 Mix the flour, salt, and water together to make a ball of dough. Roll some of the dough into a ball about 1¾ inches in diameter for the body. Squash the ball into an oval shape.

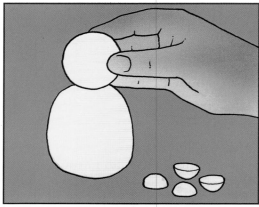

2 Roll a little more dough into a smaller ball for the head. Push the head onto the body. To make the ears and the muzzle, roll two more balls of dough and cut them in half to create four semi-circles.

3 For the ears, press two of the semi-circles on either side of the head. The muzzle is made from one semi-circle, pushed onto the teddy's face. Use cloves for the nose and eyes, and draw a smile on the face with a pin.

YOU WILL NEED
4 tablespoons plain flour
2 tablespoons salt
2 tablespoons water
3 cloves and a pin
Birthday cake candle
Cookie sheet
Paintbrush and poster paints
Craft varnish (from craft store)

4 To make the arms, roll the dough into two sausage shapes and press these onto the sides of the body. Make a small dough bow and press this onto the side of teddy's neck.

5 With the candle, make a hole in the top of the bear's head. Remove the candle and ask an adult to help you bake the teddy in a cool oven at 250°F for six hours. Paint and varnish the bear when it is cool.

SAFETY TIP: *Make sure an adult helps you when using the oven.*

MRS. TEASEL HEDGEHOG

Collect some teasels growing wild in the countryside, and use them to make this cute Mrs. Hedgehog. She is perfect as a gift, or you could make several to sell at a fund-raising event or school fair.

1 To make the dress, cut the fabric into a rectangle 11 inches x 4¼ inches. Sew ribbon and lace along the long bottom edge. Fold the fabric in half, right sides together, and sew along the short edge. Sew a running stitch along the upper edge and gather up the fabric.

YOU WILL NEED
Scissors
Fabric scraps and pins
Ribbon and lace edging
Needle and thread
One large and one
   small teasel
All-purpose glue
3 cloves
Tracing paper
   and pencil
Beige felt and cotton wool
Dried flowers

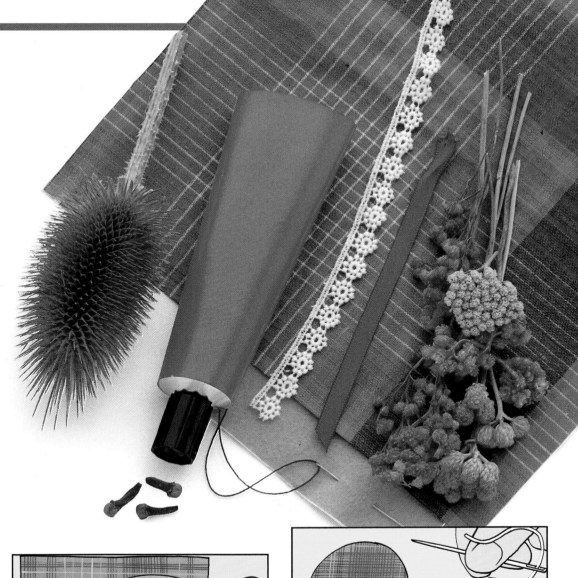

2 Slip the dress over the big teasel and glue it to the top. Glue a small teasel on top of this for the head. Glue on cloves for the eyes and nose.

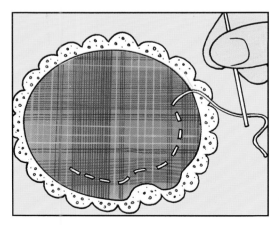

3 To make the bonnet, cut a circle from fabric 5½ inches in diameter. Sew lace around the edge of the circle. Sew a running stitch around the circle, ¾ inch from the rim. Gather up the thread to form the bonnet. Put the bonnet on the head.

4 Using a pencil, trace the sleeve and paw patterns on page 95 and cut them out. Pin the sleeve pattern onto the fabric and the paw pattern onto the felt. Cut out two sleeves and two paws.

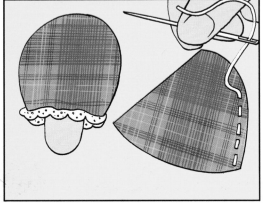

5 Fold the sleeves in half, right sides facing, and sew along the seam. Turn the sleeves right side out, and sew lace around the lower edge. Fill the sleeves with cotton wool. Place the paw in the sleeve. Gather up the sleeve around the paw and sew the fabric to the paw to secure. Glue the sleeves to the body. Glue a posy of dried flowers to the paws.

EASTER EGG TREE

This special Easter egg tree is fun and easy to make, and looks very cheerful when the eggshell baskets are filled with brightly colored flowers on Easter day. As a treat, fill the eggshells with miniature chocolate eggs instead.

YOU WILL NEED
Flower pot
Crêpe paper
All-purpose glue
Soil and moss
Branch
Blunt knife
Eggs
Ribbon
Water
Fresh flowers

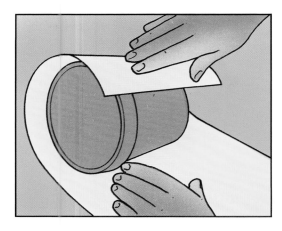

1 Cover a medium-sized flower pot with crêpe paper. Carefully glue the paper in place inside the pot and underneath.

2 Fill the pot with soil and plant into it a small branch to make the tree. Place moss on top of the soil, around the "trunk" of the tree.

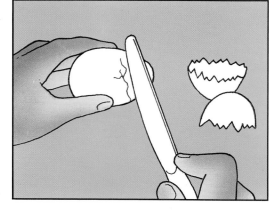

3 Using a blunt knife, gently tap around the middle of the eggs to crack them. You may want an adult to help you with this. Collect the insides of the eggs in a bowl and allow the shells to dry.

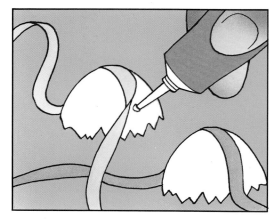

4 Glue a length of narrow ribbon around the eggshells as shown. Tie in a bow around a "branch" on your tree.

5 To decorate, pour a little water into the eggshells and carefully add a few small flowers.

PRETTY GIFT TAGS

Pressing flowers is an easy and enjoyable project. On page 12, we show you how to do this. Here, we have used the flowers to make beautiful gift tags to add a special touch to a plainly wrapped gift.

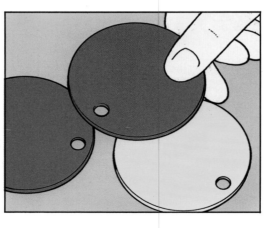

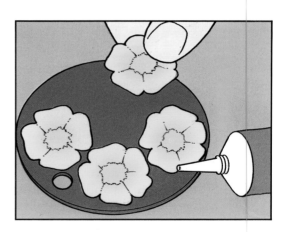

1 Cut circles and ovals from colored poster board and punch a hole in the top.

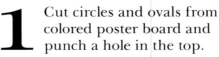

2 Arrange some pressed flowers on the gift tags. Glue the flowers in place.

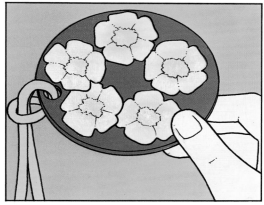

3 Thread narrow ribbon through the hole in the tags and tie it in a small knot.

4 Make some tags a little different by adding a small bow. To do this, make a few little bows from ribbon and glue them to the top of the tags.

YOU WILL NEED

Scissors
Colored poster board
Hole punch
Pressed flowers
All-purpose glue
Ribbon

HAIRY EGG HEADS

Here's a novel way to grow garden cress!
Save eggshells to make these funny hairy
egg heads. When the garden cress has
grown, mix it with chopped eggs to make
a delicious sandwich filling.

YOU WILL NEED
Empty eggshells
Felt-tip pens
Cotton wool
Garden cress (pepper grass)
   seeds
Egg carton

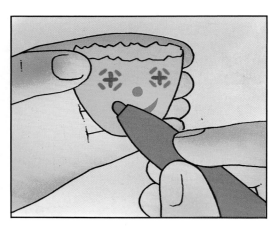

1 Wash and dry the eggshells.
Draw a funny or scary face on
each one with felt-tip pens.

2 Dampen some cotton with a
little water and gently press
it into the eggshells.

3 Carefully sprinkle just a few
of the garden cress seeds
onto the dampened cotton.

4 Stand the egg heads on a sunny window ledge in an egg carton. Make sure that the cotton does not dry out. After a few days the seeds will sprout and grow "hair"!

DRIED FLOWER GIFTWRAP

Simple dried flowers can transform a plainly wrapped gift. Use grasses and flowers you have gathered and dried yourself or buy them from a local florist or supermarket.

1 Wrap your presents neatly with shiny giftwrap, or place them in a pretty giftbag.

2 For a large square or rectangular present, arrange the dried flowers on top. When you are happy with the design, glue the flowers in position.

3 To decorate a small gift, wrap narrow ribbon around it, and slip a tiny spray of dried flowers under the ribbon.

4 For the giftbag, gather together a small bunch of dried flowers and tie them together with a ribbon. Finish with a bow and glue the posy to the bag at a slight angle.

YOU WILL NEED
Plain, shiny giftwrap
  or giftbag
Scotch tape
Scissors
Dried flowers and grasses
All-purpose glue
Ribbon

POT-POURRI HEARTS

These delightful heart-shaped sachets are made from scraps of fabric and net. Fill the hearts with fragrant pot-pourri which can be bought from a drug store or beauty shop. The pot-pourri looks very pretty in the lacy hearts.

YOU WILL NEED
Tracing paper and pencil
Scissors
Lacy net fabric
Plain fabric
Pins
Pinking shears
Needle and thread
Pot-pourri
10 inch-narrow ribbon
4 inches of ⅝-inch
    wide ribbon

1 Using a pencil, trace the heart pattern on page 95. Cut out this pattern.

2 Pin the pattern on to both the lace and the fabric and carefully cut around the shape with pinking shears.

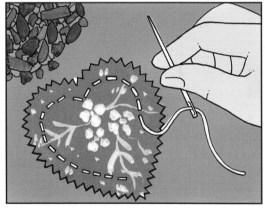

3 Sew together the lace and fabric hearts leaving a small gap at one edge. Pour some pot-pourri into the sachet and finish sewing around the heart. Make a hanging loop from the narrow ribbon and sew this to the top of the heart.

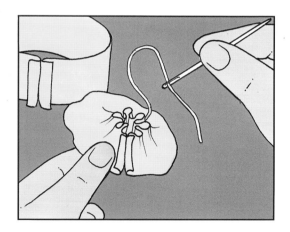

4 To make a little rosette, sew the ends of the length of wide ribbon together to make a circle. Sew a running stitch along one edge and gather up the thread tightly to form a little rosette. Sew the rosette to the front of the heart.

PRINTED EASTER EGGS

Use leaves, ferns, or flowers to decorate eggs for Easter. The finished eggs can be placed in a large, attractive bowl, or threaded onto ribbon to make a pretty hanging decoration.

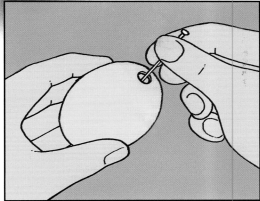

1 Gently poke both ends of the egg with a needle to make a small hole. Make one hole ¼ inch wide and the other ⅜ inch wide.

YOU WILL NEED
Eggs
Needle
Bowl
Fabric dye
Rubber gloves
Poster paints
Paintbrush
Small ferns and leaves

3 Ask an adult to help you prepare the fabric dye following the instructions on the package. Wearing rubber gloves, hold the egg in the dye solution for a few minutes, then take it out and leave it in the egg carton or another bowl to dry.

4 Paint the ferns and leaves with poster paint and press them on to the egg, creating lovely patterns as you do so. Allow the eggs to dry thoroughly before using them.

2 Insert the needle into the egg to break the yoke. Hold the egg over a bowl and blow gently through the small hole to empty the contents of the egg into the bowl. You may want an adult to help you with this.

SAFETY TIP: *Ask an adult to help you prepare the fabric dye.*

SHELL CREATURES

Create these cute little pets from shells you have collected on a trip to the beach. Limpet shells make great tortoises, while smaller shells can be turned into mice and snails.

YOU WILL NEED
Shells
All-purpose glue
Stick-on "joggle" eyes
   (from craft store)
Embroidery thread

2 When you are happy with the animal shapes, stick the shells together with a strong, all-purpose glue.

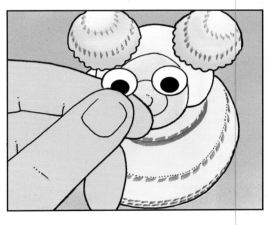

3 Glue on "joggle" eyes where necessary. For example, tortoises and snails may not need eyes.

1 Hold the shells against one another to see which would make interesting creatures.

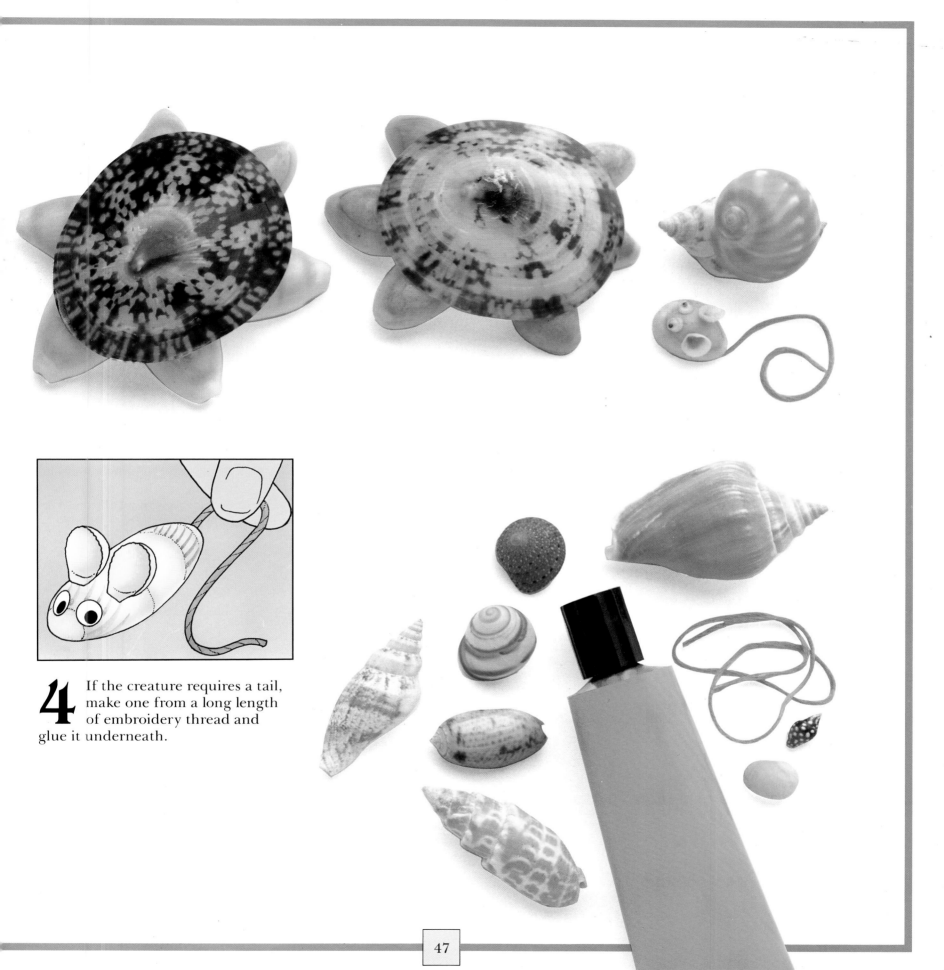

4 If the creature requires a tail, make one from a long length of embroidery thread and glue it underneath.

CORK COASTERS

Practical cork drink coasters can be transformed into a perfect Christmas or birthday gift by adding some pretty dried strawflowers for decoration.

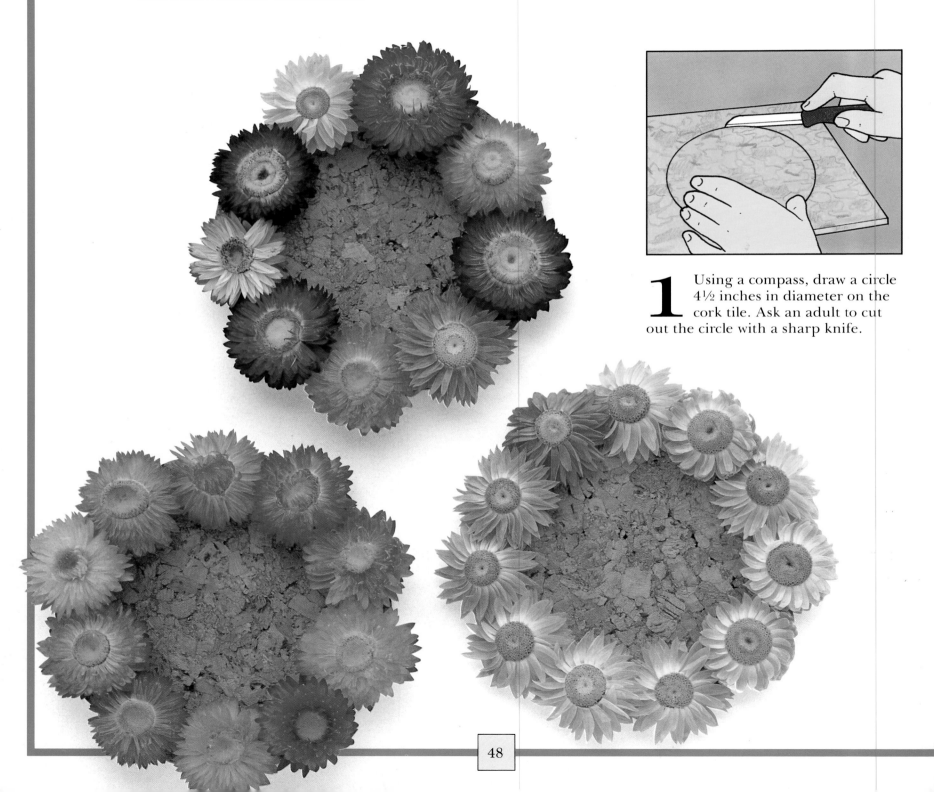

1 Using a compass, draw a circle 4½ inches in diameter on the cork tile. Ask an adult to cut out the circle with a sharp knife.

4 Glue the flower heads securely in position. Allow the coasters to dry before use.

3 Arrange the flower heads in a ring around the edge of the cork coaster.

2 With scissors, cut off the stems of the dried flowers close to the heads.

YOU WILL NEED
Compass and pencil
Cork tile
   (from craft or
   hardware store)
Sharp knife
Dried flowers
Scissors
All-purpose glue

SAFETY TIP: *Make sure an adult helps you when using a sharp knife.*

DRIED FLOWER POSY

A selection of dried flowers tied together with a brightly colored ribbon makes a perfect birthday present. Make the posy extra special by adding a lace doily.

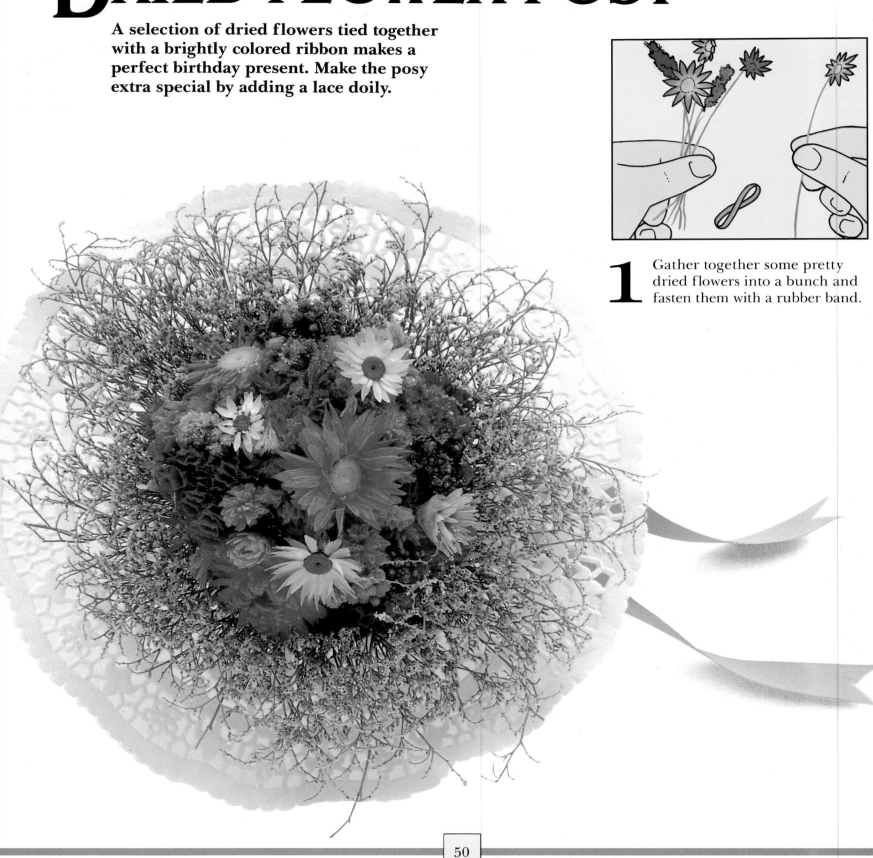

1 Gather together some pretty dried flowers into a bunch and fasten them with a rubber band.

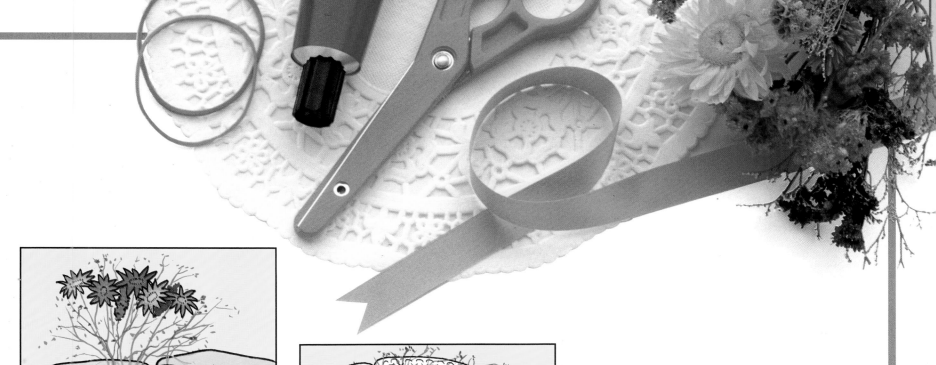

2 Put sprigs of sea lavender around the bunch and fasten the whole posy with the other rubber band.

3 Cut a hole in the center of a doily. Push the stems of the posy through the hole.

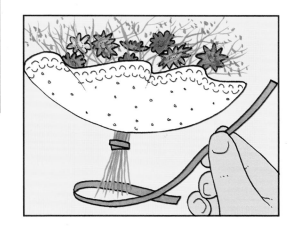

4 Dab a little glue to stick the doily to the stems of the posy. Tie a ribbon around the posy and finish with a pretty bow.

YOU WILL NEED
Dried flowers and
  sea lavender
2 rubber bands
Paper doily
Scissors
All-purpose glue
Ribbon

KNOT GARDENS

In Elizabethan England, wealthy people planted their herbs in strict geometric patterns. These were called knot gardens. You can create your own knot garden collage using natural materials such as beans, peas, and lentils.

SAFETY TIP: *Don't eat the dried beans – they could give you an upset stomach.*

2 With a pencil, lightly draw a geometric shape on the poster board. If you prefer, copy the designs shown here.

YOU WILL NEED
Scissors
Poster board
Pencil
All-purpose glue
Colored lentils
Split peas
Aduki or other small oval
   dried beans
Pearl barley

3 Starting at the center of the pattern, spread a little glue on the poster board and press some of the pieces in position.

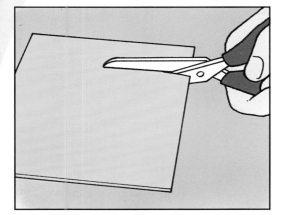

1 Using scissors, cut out a rectangle of poster board 6 inches x 6 inches.

4 Continue working outward, spreading the glue in sections, until you have completely filled in the design.

SHELL BOXES

Shells gathered from the beach can be used to decorate many things. Here, they adorn the top of a plain wooden box, turning it into a pretty jewelry holder.

YOU WILL NEED

Old newspaper
Poster paints
  diluted with water
Paintbrush
Wooden box
Shells
All-purpose glue

1 Cover your work surface with old newspaper. Mix the paint with a little water to make a thin, runny solution. Paint the box and allow it to dry.

2 Arrange the shells in a pretty pattern on the box lid. Position the largest shells first.

3 When you are happy with your design, carefully glue the shells in place.

4 Leave the sides of the box plain or glue on a few small shells at random.

GOLDEN GIFTWRAP

Christmas giftwrap can be expensive to buy. This year wrap your presents in brown paper, but add a pretty arrangement of natural items, such as pine cones and leaves and a touch of gold paint.

1 Neatly wrap a present with brown parcel paper in the usual way.

4 You can also add loops or bows of giftwrap ribbon and glue them among the trimmings.

3 Put some of the pine cones and other items on newspaper and paint them with gold paint. Allow to dry. Arrange different pieces on the gift and glue in place.

2 To make a gold-trimmed gift, tie gold giftwrap ribbon around the parcel, as shown.

YOU WILL NEED
Brown parcel paper
Scissors and scotch tape
Gold giftwrap ribbon
Pine cones and seed pods
Dried leaves and grasses
Teasels
Cinnamon sticks
Tree bark
Gold poster paint
Paintbrush
Old newspaper
All-purpose glue

DRIED FLOWER JEWELRY

Make this pretty collection of summer jewelry using a selection of colorful dried flowers. Make a matching set of hair and fashion accessories or create your own designs to match your outfits.

1 To protect the most delicate dried flowers, paint them with a layer of craft varnish.

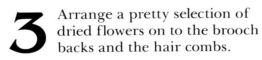

3 Arrange a pretty selection of dried flowers on to the brooch backs and the hair combs.

2 For the earrings, glue a single flower to the earring backs. Leave to dry in a safe place.

4 When you are happy with your design glue the flowers securely in position.

YOU WILL NEED

Dried flowers
Clip-on earring backs
Brooch backs
Hair combs
Barrettes
All-purpose glue
Craft varnish

FRUITY POTATO PRINTS

Potato prints can produce very professional results. Use them to print notepaper, gift tags, and envelopes. Wash and re-use the same potato for a different color, or make up several shapes on a few potatoes.

YOU WILL NEED
Washed potatoes
Sharp knife
Felt-tip pen
Paintbrush
Poster paints
Colored writing paper
Hole punch
Ribbon

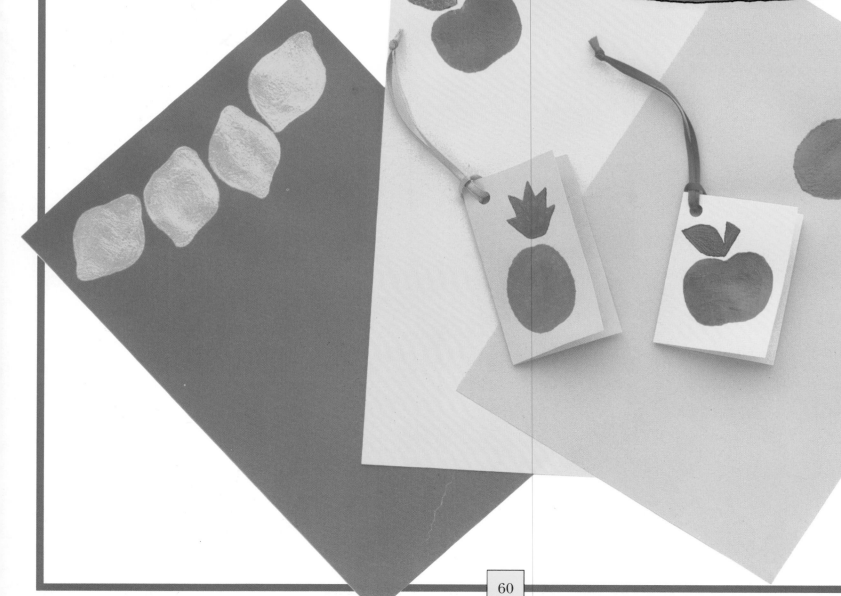

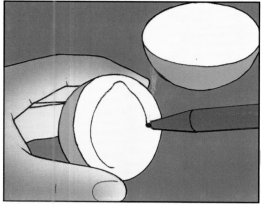

1 Using a sharp knife, cut a potato in half. Draw the fruit on one half with a felt-tip pen.

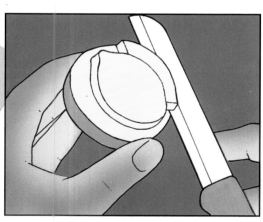

2 Holding the knife upright, cut around the outline of the fruit you have drawn, then cut away the potato around the fruit, leaving a raised, flat shape.

3 With a paintbrush, apply a fairly thick layer of paint to the raised fruit shape, then press it firmly onto the paper.

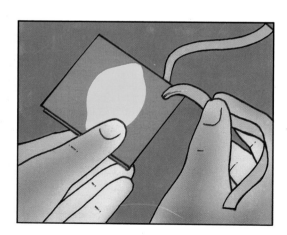

4 You can print a motif at the top of a sheet of writing paper or fold the paper in half to make a notelet and print onto it a group of fruits.

5 To make gift tags, cut a rectangle of paper and fold it in half. Punch a hole at the top of the tag and thread with ribbon.

SAFETY TIP: *Make sure an adult helps you when using a sharp knife.*

POT-POURRI BASKETS

These pretty little baskets make ideal gifts when filled with pot-pourri, especially when you have made your own mixture. Gather together dried flower heads, spices, leaves, and petals, and add a few drops of essential oil to enhance the natural smell of the ingredients.

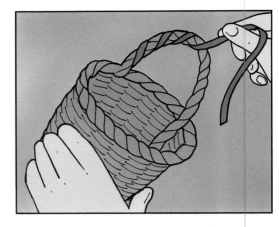

1 Wrap ribbon around the handle of the basket and weave some more through the rim if the basket weave is fairly open.

2 In a bowl, combine petals and flowerheads, bay leaves, spices (such as crushed cinnamon sticks), and a few drops of essential oil; rose, sandalwood or lavender smell wonderful.

YOU WILL NEED
Small basket
Ribbon
Bowl
Dried flowers, petals, flowerheads, bay leaves, cinnamon sticks
Essential oil (from drug store or beauty shop)

3 Fill the baskets with two or three handfuls of the pot-pourri mixture.

4 Tie miniature posies of dried flowers to the handle of the basket with ribbon bows.

FLOWER PAPERWEIGHTS

No one will believe you have made these wonderful paperweights. Although you have to buy the glass and varnish from craft stores, you can pick and press your own flowers following the instructions for Pressed Flower Cards on page 12.

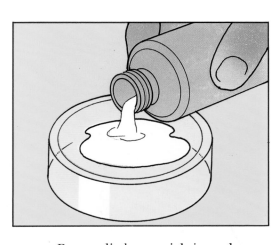

1 Pour a little varnish into the recess of the paperweight. Move the base from side to side to spread the varnish evenly.

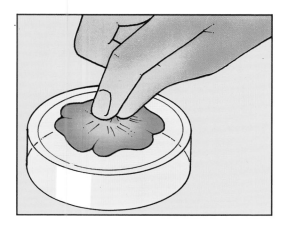

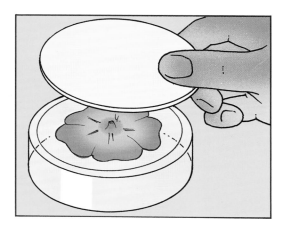

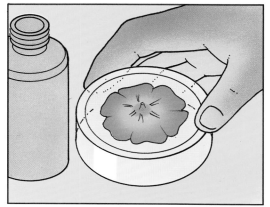

2 Carefully place a pressed flower face down in the varnish. Pour a little more varnish over the top of the flower to cover it.

3 Move the paperweight again from side to side to spread the varnish. Allow the varnish to harden for four to five days.

4 Cut a piece of poster board to fit in the recess of the paperweight. Finish the paperweight by glueing a piece of felt to the base.

YOU WILL NEED
Glass paperweight
    with recessed
        base (from craft store)
Craft varnish
    (from craft store)
Pressed flowers
Scissors
Poster board
Felt
All-purpose glue

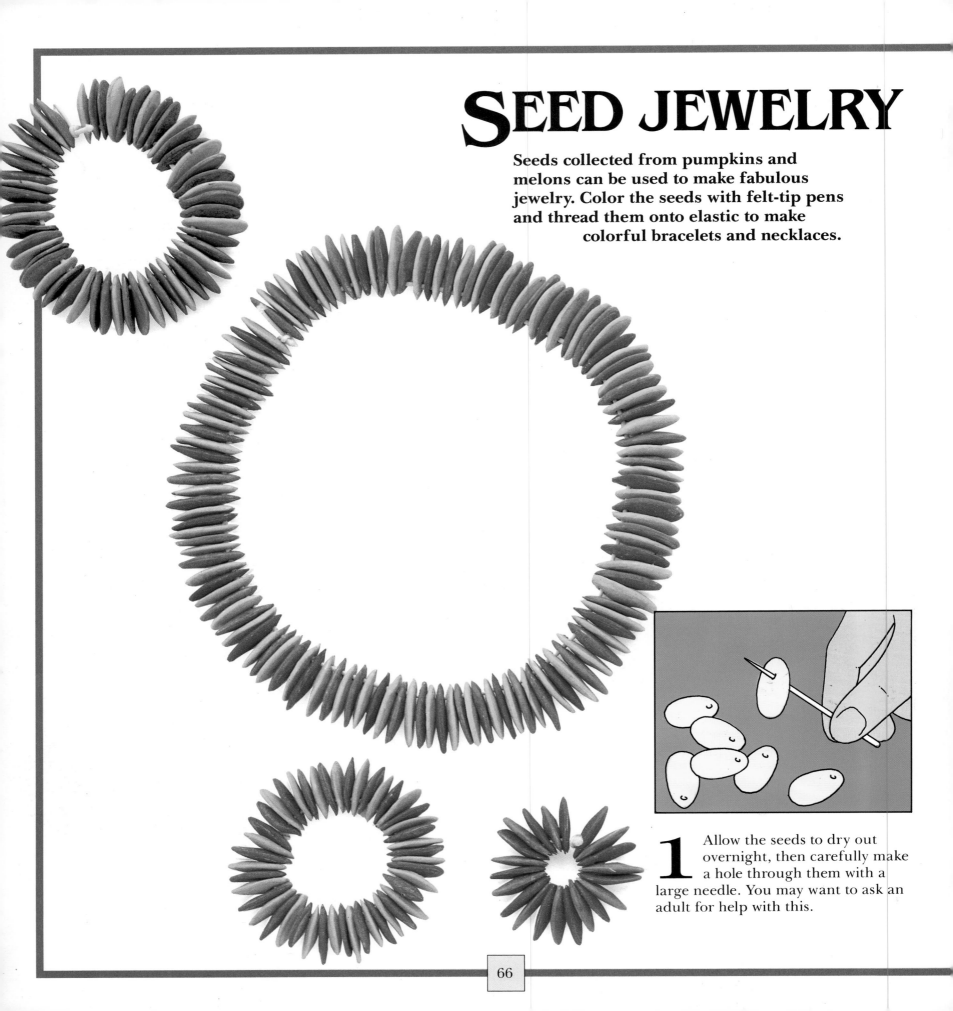

SEED JEWELRY

Seeds collected from pumpkins and melons can be used to make fabulous jewelry. Color the seeds with felt-tip pens and thread them onto elastic to make colorful bracelets and necklaces.

1 Allow the seeds to dry out overnight, then carefully make a hole through them with a large needle. You may want to ask an adult for help with this.

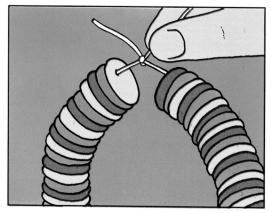

4 Fasten the ends of the elastic together with a tight knot. Shuffle the seeds along the elastic to hide the knot.

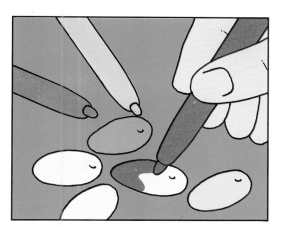

2 Color one side of the seeds with felt-tip pens. Allow the seeds to dry, then color the other sides too.

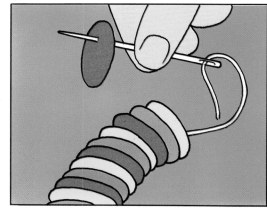

3 Thread the seeds onto the elastic until it is long enough for a necklace, bracelet, or pony-tail band.

YOU WILL NEED
Pumpkin or melon seeds
Large needle
Waterproof felt-tip pens
Hat elastic

STRING COLLAGE

This stylish box would make a perfect container for jewelry. The string can be glued on in any design you like, but it is best to keep the shapes simple.

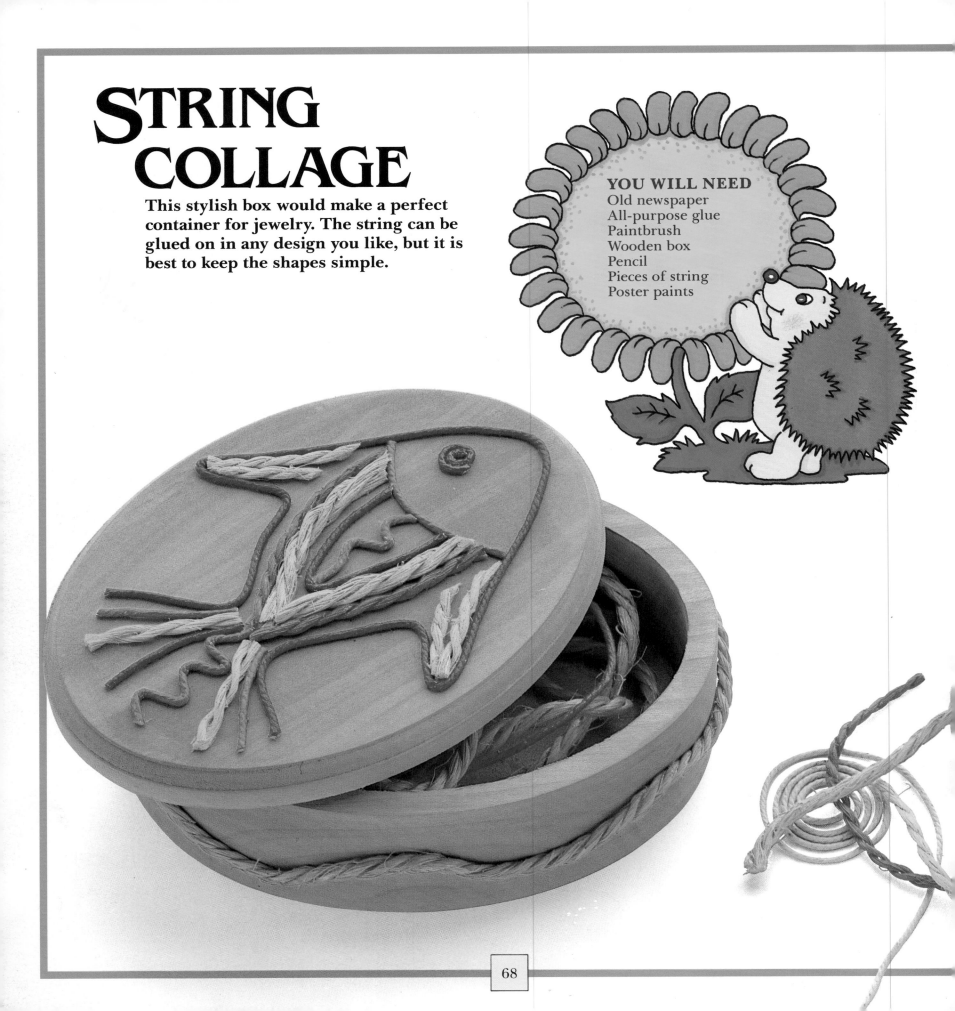

YOU WILL NEED
Old newspaper
All-purpose glue
Paintbrush
Wooden box
Pencil
Pieces of string
Poster paints

1 Cover your work surface with old newspaper. Mix together a thin solution of paint and water. Paint the box and allow it to dry.

2 With a pencil, lightly draw a simple fish shape on the lid and a wiggly line around the side of the box.

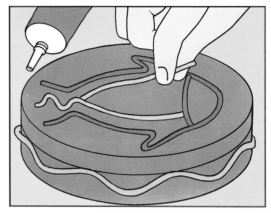

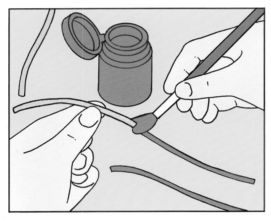

3 Paint the string with undiluted poster paints and leave it to dry. Spread glue along the pencil lines and press a length of string on top.

4 Fill in the fish with straight and wiggly lines of string. Glue in place on the box. Coil narrow string tightly to make an eye and glue it to the fish.

BLOOMING BOOKMARKS

Pressing flowers and leaves is fun and you can use them to make all sorts of original decorations and gifts, such as these pretty bookmarks. Always use freshly picked flowers and choose ones that are fairly flat as they are much easier to press.

YOU WILL NEED
Blotter paper
Heavy book
Small leaves and flowers
Tweezers and scissors
Colored poster board
All-purpose glue
Clear sticky-backed
   plastic
Ruler and ribbon

1 Open a large, heavy book and lay a sheet of blotter paper inside. Arrange small leaves and brightly colored flowers on the blotter paper.

2 Place a second sheet of blotter paper over the flowers and leaves. Close the book and leave it in a safe place.

3 After a few weeks, open the book and carefully remove the flowers with tweezers. Arrange the flowers and leaves on strips of poster board. When you are happy with the pattern, glue the flowers and leaves into place.

4 To protect the flowers, carefully cover the bookmarks with clear sticky-backed plastic film. Use a ruler to smooth out any air bubbles. Trim the edges with scissors. Glue on a small ribbon bow.

JACK-O'-LANTERN

No Halloween would be complete
without a traditional Jack-O'-Lantern.
Put a night light inside and place your
finished lantern on a window sill to
frighten away the spooks.

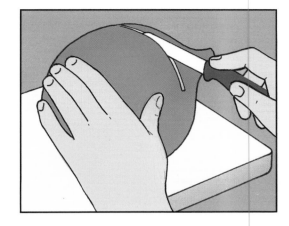

1 Cover your work surface with
old newspaper. Using a sharp
knife, slice the top off the
turnip or pumpkin. Ask an adult to
help you do this.

SAFETY TIP: *Make sure an adult helps you when using a sharp knife.*

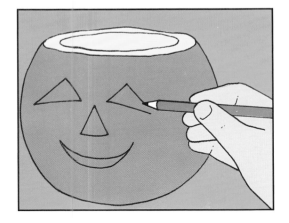

2 Spoon or cut out the inside of the turnip or pumpkin. Ask an adult to do this for you. Draw a face on the front of the vegetable with a felt-tip pen.

3 Carefully cut around the outlines on the face with a sharp knife, then push out the features from the inside.

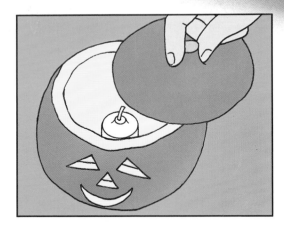

YOU WILL NEED
Old newspaper
Turnip or pumpkin
Sharp knife
Spoon
Felt-tip pen
Night light

4 Put a night light in the lantern. Ask an adult to help you light it. Put the lid on top but do not leave the lit lantern unattended.

HERBY BATH FRAGRANCES

Hang these pretty herb sachets on the bath faucet. As the water runs through the bag, the herb fragrances will be carried into the water. Use any of the herb mixtures suggested here, or make up your own combinations.

1 From the muslin, cut a 7-inch diameter circle. Place any of the herb mixtures in the center of the circle.

3 Tie the ribbon ends together in a bow so the bag can be hung on to a faucet.

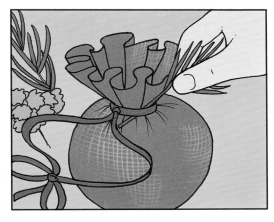

4 To finish, tuck some sprigs of herbs or lavender flowers under the ribbon.

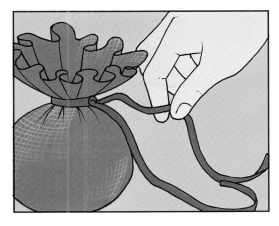

2 Add a tablespoon of bran or oatmeal as a water softener, if you wish. Gather up the fabric circle and tie a length of ribbon around the top.

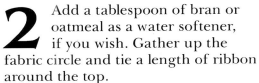

YOU WILL NEED
Dyed or natural muslin
Scissors
Bran or oatmeal
Narrow ribbon

For the herb mixtures:
Thyme and lavender
Lemon balm and rosemary
Camomile flowers
Apple mint and parsley
Sage and strawberry
   leaves

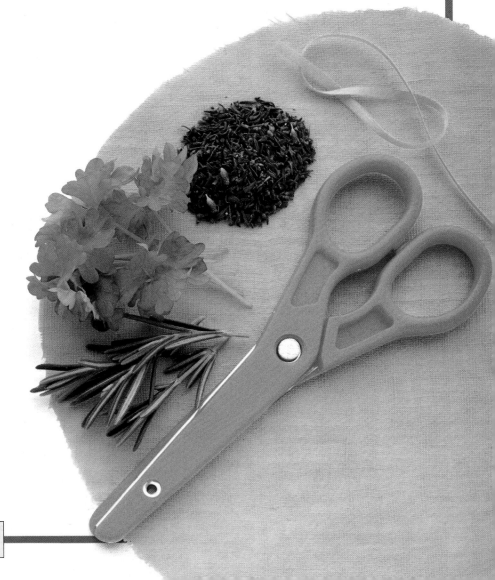

CHRISTMAS POMANDERS

These sweet-smelling pomanders are simple to make and look very festive tied up with brightly colored velvet ribbon. Make your own pot-pourri from dried flower heads and scented oils, or buy some already prepared.

YOU WILL NEED
Old newspaper
Thick paintbrush
White glue
Ball of florists' foam
Chunky pot-pourri
Scissors
Velvet ribbon
All-purpose glue
Needle and thread

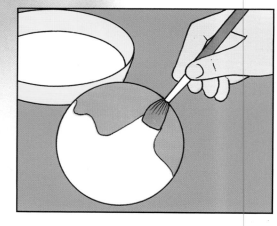

1 Cover your work surface with newspaper. Using a paintbrush, spread white glue over a ball of florists' foam. Press pot-pourri into the ball while the glue is still wet.

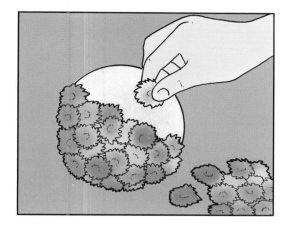

2 Make sure the ball is completely covered with pot-pourri before allowing it to dry overnight in a safe place.

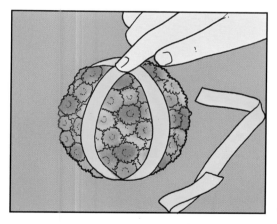

3 Cut two lengths of ribbon long enough to go around the pomander. Glue them in place.

4 Make a small ribbon loop and glue or sew this to the top of the pomander so you can hang it up.

5 For a finishing touch, make a ribbon bow and glue this to the top of the pomander.

GOLDEN TREE DECORATIONS

These elegant, golden Christmas tree decorations have been made from pine cones and ivy leaves that you can collect on a nature walk or even from your own yard.

1 Cover your work surface with old newspaper. Using a paintbrush, paint the cones and ivy leaves with gold paint. (Thin the gold paint with a little water to get a good even color.)

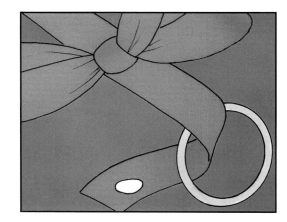

2 To make the cone decoration, cut a length of ribbon and make a big bow. Glue this to the base of the cone, as shown.

3 To make the ivy decoration, take two ivy leaves and glue them onto another length of ribbon, sticking them a little distance apart. Make two bows using a wider ribbon and glue these into position between the ivy leaves.

4 Thread the top of the ribbon through a curtain ring. Glue the end of the ribbon firmly in place behind the top bow.

YOU WILL NEED
Old newspaper
Paintbrush
Gold acrylic paint,
 diluted with water
Pine cones
Ivy leaves
Scissors
Ribbon in two widths
All-purpose glue
Curtain rings

WINTER SKIERS

Made from fir cones, these little skiers
can decorate a cake, the
Christmas table or coast down
the branches of your Christmas
tree. The materials here make
one skier.

YOU WILL NEED
Old newspaper
Pine cone and a clove
2 wooden skewers
Acrylic paints and paintbrush
1¼ inch cotton ball
   (from craft store)
Cup of black tea
All-purpose glue
Felt-tip pens
Felt scraps and scissors
Colored poster board
2 pipe cleaners

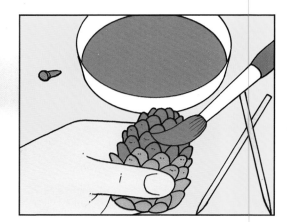

1 Cover your work surface with
old newspaper. Paint the
pine cone, clove,
and skewers with
acrylic paint.
Color the cotton
ball using a brush
dipped in black
tea. When dry, glue
the cotton ball onto
the pine cone.

2 Push the clove into the cotton ball as a nose. Draw on eyes and a mouth with felt-tip pens. For the scarf, cut a felt strip and snip a fringe into the ends. Tie it around the neck.

3 To make the hat, cut a circle from felt 4 inches in diameter. Then cut it in half. Glue this into a cone shape and attach it to the head.

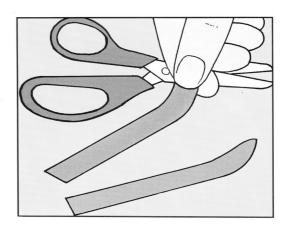

4 Cut two pointed poster board strips for skis. Pull the points up between your finger and thumb to curve them upwards. Glue them underneath the pine cone.

5 For the arms, cut two pipe cleaners into 5½-inch lengths, twist them together, and wrap them around the cone. Bend the ends of the pipe cleaners around the skewers.

CHRISTMAS RAFFIA WREATH

Natural raffia and flowers make a beautiful wreath that you can hang up any time of year. But with the addition of shiny ribbon and baubles, you can create the perfect decoration for Christmas time.

YOU WILL NEED
Natural raffia
Narrow red giftwrap ribbon
Scissors
Masking tape
5 small red ball ornaments
Red and pink dried flowers
All-purpose glue

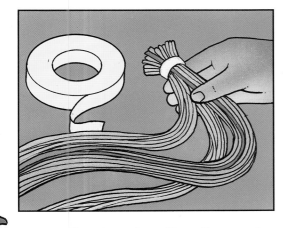

1 Cut three bundles of natural raffia 20 inches long and one 20-inch length of giftwrap ribbon. Bind the bundles of raffia and the ribbon together at one end with masking tape.

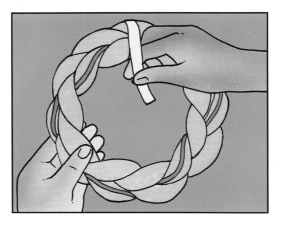

2 Braid the raffia and giftwrap ribbon and when complete overlap the ends to form a circle. Bind the ends together with masking tape.

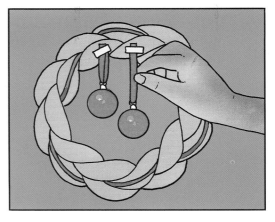

3 Thread three of the balls onto lengths of ribbon and hang them inside the wreath with masking tape. Glue flower heads to the top of the baubles.

4 Choose some long, trailing dried flowers and glue them on either side of the wreath at the top. Glue a few flower heads and the other two balls at the top of the wreath to hide the masking tape.

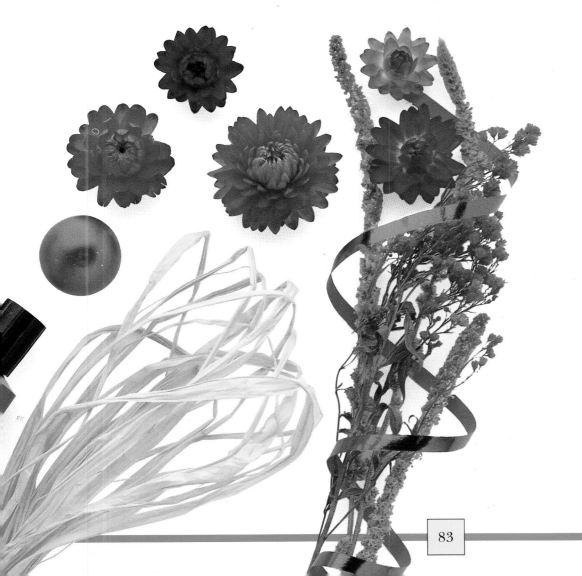

STRAW ANGELS

These straw angels will look great hanging from your Christmas tree. Give each angel a tiny posy of dried flowers or a handful of pine cones to hold.

1 Cut the heads from a bunch of dried barley. Strip off the leaves and soften the stems in a pot of warm water for two hours.

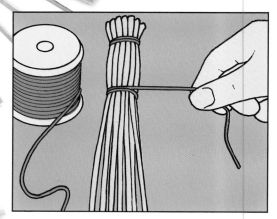

2 Cut 12 stems 7 inches long. Hold the stems together and tie red thread around one end, and again 1 inch away to make the head.

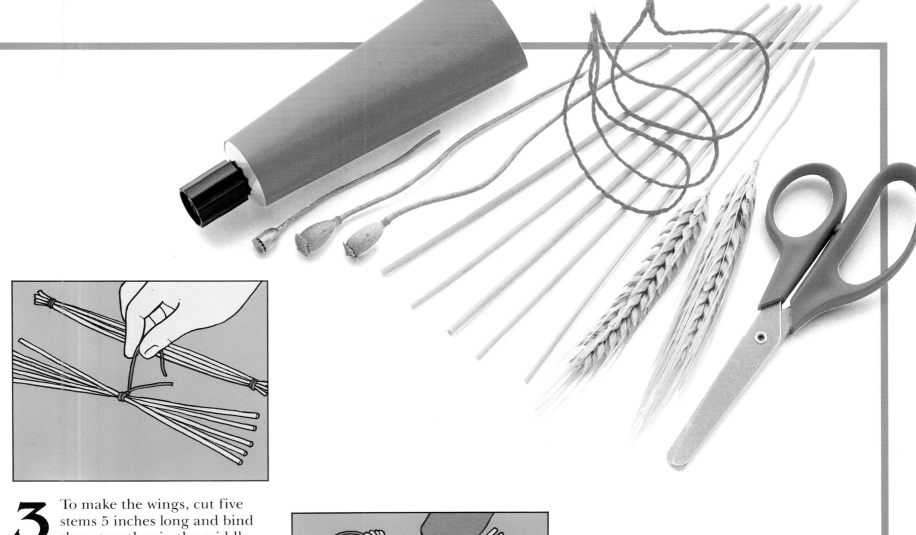

3 To make the wings, cut five stems 5 inches long and bind them together in the middle. For the arms, cut three stems 5 inches long and bind them together at each end with red thread.

5 Bend the arms together in front and glue the hands together. To finish, make a loop from thread and glue it to the back of the head.

4 Slip the arms and wings between the long stems of the angel's body and bind directly beneath to make the waist.

YOU WILL NEED
Scissors
Dried barley or wheat
Pot of warm water
Red embroidery thread
All-purpose glue
Dried flowers
Pine cones

SANTA AND HIS HELPERS

Make a group of jolly Christmas characters from salt-dough – just flour, salt, and water mixed together. Paint them in bright, cheerful colors and hang them from the Christmas tree.

YOU WILL NEED
2 cups plain flour
1 cup salt
1 cup water
Rolling pin
Gingerbread man cookie
    cutter
Blunt knife and pencil
Poster paints
    Craft varnish
    (from craft store)
    Narrow ribbon

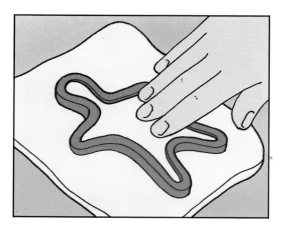

1 Mix the flour, salt, and water together to make a firm dough. Roll out to ⅜ inch thick and cut out the characters with a cookie cutter.

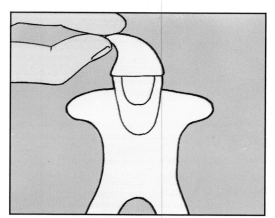

2 Mold a triangle for the beard and hat; flatten and press these to the head. Bend over the tip of the hat for the elves.

3 Cut out strips of dough for the belt, the cuffs on the sleeves, and Santa's fur trim. Roll two balls of dough for the shoes and two small balls for the buttons. Now roll out small pieces of dough to make the eyes and nose. Press all the pieces into place. Make a hole in the tip of the hat to thread the ribbon through later.

4 Draw a smile on the beard with the point of the pencil. Make little marks on Santa's fur trim and each of the beards using a blunt knife.

5 Ask an adult to help you bake the models in an oven for about four hours at 250°F. When the models are cool, paint them in bright colors. Allow to dry before varnishing. Hang each one on the tree with a piece of ribbon.

SAFETY TIP: *Make sure an adult helps you when using the oven.*

CHRISTMAS LOG

This Christmas, make a bright and
cheery table centerpiece from leaves
and bark collected on a forest walk.
Make sure that the bark is quite dry
before using it.

1 With a blunt knife, cut a slice
of florists' foam about
2½ inches thick. Glue the foam
on top of the bark and when dry, slice
away the corners, as shown.

2 Dampen the foam and push a candle holder into it. Put the candle into the holder.

3 Insert sprigs of holly, some with berries, into the foam around the candle holder.

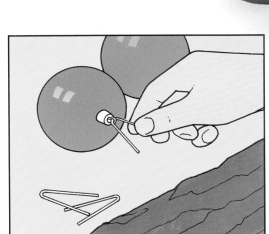

4 Bend a length of wire in half and push it through the hanging loop of the ball ornament. Tuck the baubles in among the sprigs of holly.

YOU WILL NEED
Blunt knife
Florists' foam
All-purpose glue
Tree bark
Candle holder
Red candle
Sprigs of holly
Florists' wire
Green ball ornaments

RAFFIA NAPKIN RINGS

These brightly colored napkin rings are made from cardboard and natural raffia. The finished rings are stunning and no one would realize that you didn't buy them from a fancy store.

YOU WILL NEED
Natural raffia
(from craft store)
Fabric dye
Old newspaper
Cardboard tube
Scissors
All-purpose glue

SAFETY TIP: *Ask an adult to help you prepare the fabric dye.*

90

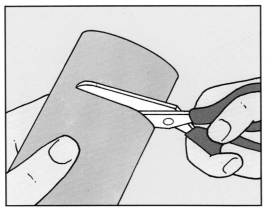

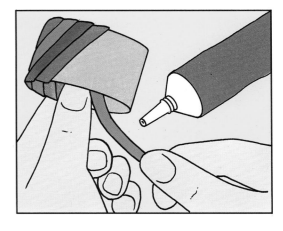

2 Remove the raffia, rinse it well, and allow it to dry on old newspaper. Cut a cardboard tube into 1½ inch lengths.

3 Bind one of the cardboard rings diagonally with the colored raffia, glueing the ends securely inside.

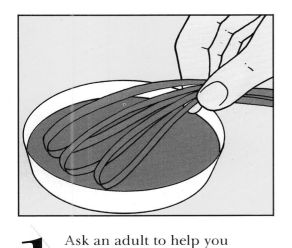

1 Ask an adult to help you prepare the fabric dye following the instructions on the package. Hold lengths of raffia in the dye for a few minutes.

4 Another way to decorate a ring is to wind the raffia around it horizontally. Glue the ends inside the ring.

PATTERNS

The following pages show the patterns you will need to make some of the projects in the book. To find out how to copy a pattern, follow the step-by-step instructions given for each project.

You may want to make a pattern that you can keep to use again. To do this, trace over the outline of the pattern with a pencil. Turn your tracing over and place it on a piece of poster board. Rub firmly over the outline with a pencil. The image will appear on the poster board. Cut out the shape. If you keep this pattern in a safe place, you can use it time and time again.

COCKATIEL COLLAGE

Page **14**

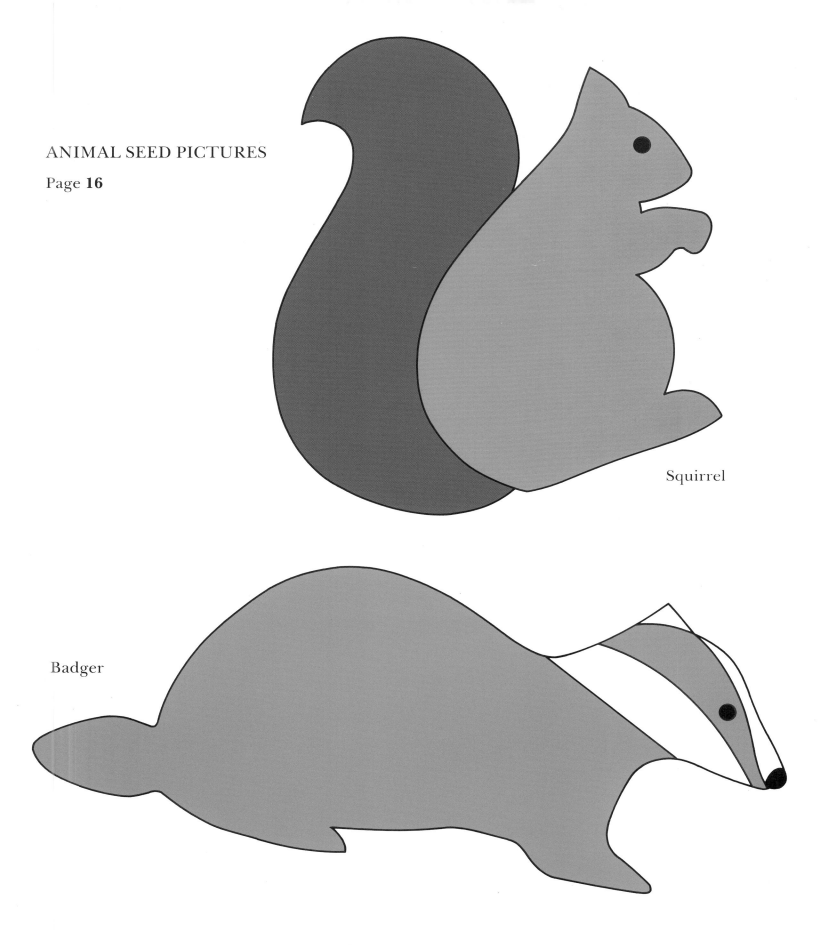

ANIMAL SEED PICTURES

Page **16**

Squirrel

Badger

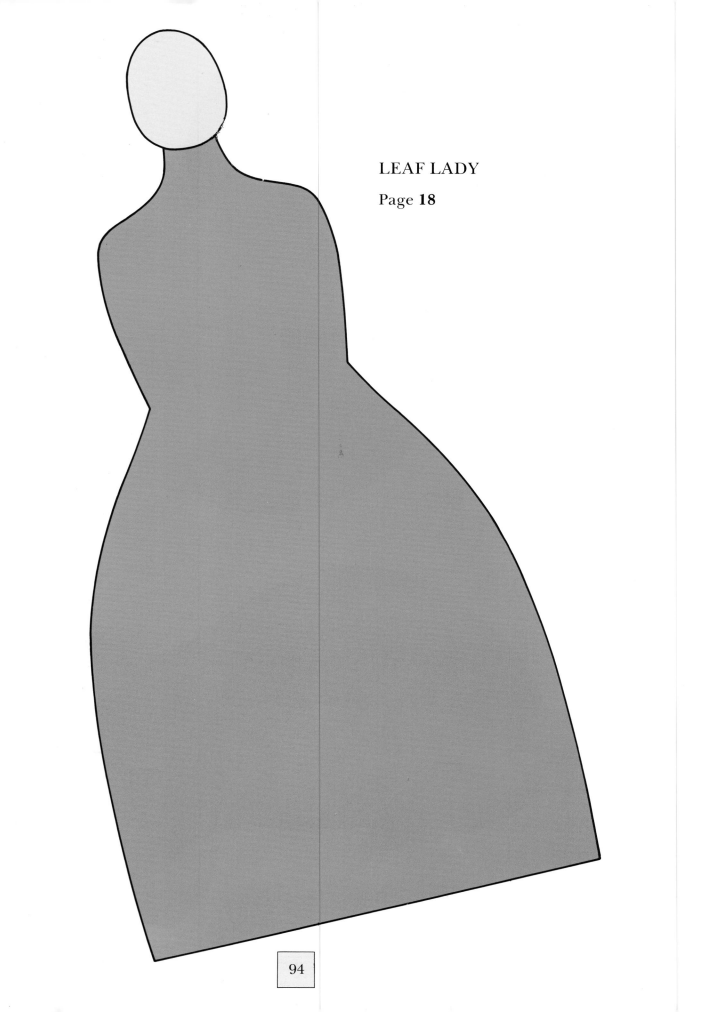

LEAF LADY

Page **18**

MRS. TEASEL HEDGEHOG

Page **32**

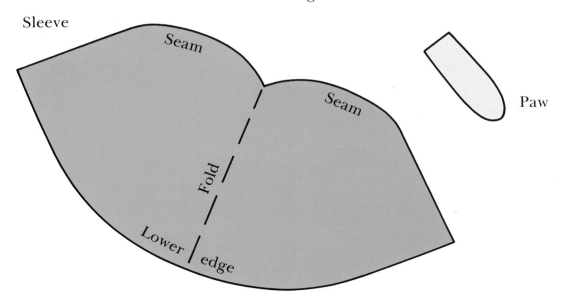

Sleeve

Seam

Seam

Fold

Lower edge

Paw

POT-POURRI HEARTS

Page **42**

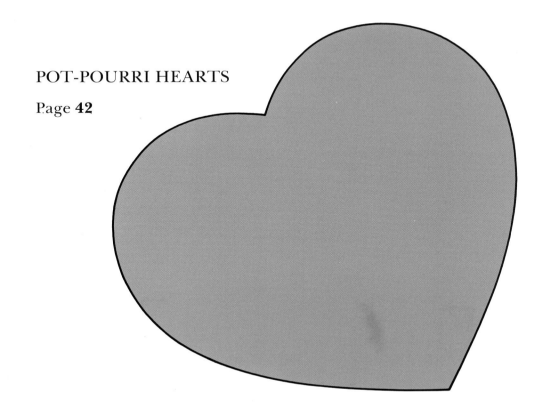

INDEX